LIKE THIS, LIKE THAT

Like This, Like That

POEMS BY

L I B B Y   W A G N E R

LOST HORSE PRESS

SANDPOINT, IDAHO 2002

Library of Congress Cataloging-in-Publication-Data

Wagner, Libby

   Like this, like that: poems / by Libby Wagner

           p. cm.

ISBN 0-9668612-9-9

I. Title.

PS3623.A396 L55 2002

811'.6—dc21

                    2002005390

for
LaVerne Rush Moorman
1913-2002
in memory

CONTENTS

Like This, Like That

Asking Eve

What I remember most
was the quality of light.
Fused light filtered
through cedar, ginkgo, alder.
Shadows deepening our reflections
in glassy water, bits of our faces
in shallow creek beds. It was clear.
We knew who we were.
Every day began with sunlight,
so we rose and walked about
naming things: *beautiful orchid,*
raspberry, tarantula. It felt
like good work. We weren't lying
about, no matter what anyone tries
to say. Paradise was no bargain.
But there were colors with names
I cannot even imagine now.
And every night, the moon,
sifting through the canopy.

Of course, he was the first
muse. And I trusted him,
not knowing any other way.
I tried on my skin, my hair,
billowing like silk scarves,
fluttering, and I danced. We

couldn't get enough
of each other, our days filled
with laughter, the recording
and collecting of data, our nights
brimming with the smell of
each other and jasmine.

In some ways, he was so good.
He never asked for direction,
felt certain of his task, our purpose
together. I had so many questions,
words like butterflies, *there* no,
there. I simply had to ask,
to know. And that
was that.

It's true, everything changed
then. His heart closed like a fist.
We became difficult, and cold.
It was as if we could not speak
one another's language.
After a while, I knew I could
find my own way, but I stayed.
Guilt? Loyalty? Had we named
those yet? No, I stayed because
we fucked, and I knew by then
to live in my body would allow me
to finally leave my body.

There was no serpent. No evil
darkness in me, only the knowledge
that Paradise was brief, and the rest
would be the good work,
the cataloging of my muscles
and bones, the stretch of a dancer,
the drawing from the well, and
some great time after, the poems
written before the last breath,
the only breath I would take.

Back to the Muse

Finally, I do not say
oh my god did he just drool on me?
or when he kneads my ass like that,
lifts me up off the floor, walks over
to the mirror to watch me:
head thrown back, hair tangled
in his fist, hoisted up
on his own hips. Here I don't
find words for *I bet he's got a great*
view of my thighs dimpling as
 we ram our bones together like this.

Who cares? I'm exactly
where I should be. Exactly.

Look, I don't want to write sex
poems anymore. No more poems
of the body. I want nature.

After all this time. The garden.

Oh, to call green what it is, to taste
the tartest lemon. I have my eyes, my tongue,
my ears. I'll get back to you
on Nirvana.
Now is worth it. *Now*
I step into my skin.

You couldn't tell Adam, First muse.
Purveyor of The Big Ache.
Good Eve, who tried on her skin.
She had so many questions,
words like butterflies, *there* one minute,
then gone, semen spilled
on her belly, pooling in her navel.

Who takes you that way?

Heart like a closed fist, he loves my food,
my hair, the small of my back.
Uses big words to say so, reads me
the dictionary in bed. I know what
the fuck he's talking about:

I've been to years of college and I should know better,
but I love it when he calls me baby.

Baby. First time, bent double over
the desk, hands splayed out
on the veneer, hip bones bruising
up against the stiff edge. The body's
presentation. The body's communion.

This man waits up for me.
Around every corner, lifts me up
so I feel the cold slap of my
legs against the tile counter. I keep

changing my address and telephone number.

Every time I write my thighs ache.

We've got to talk about this, I say, because
you're interfering with my work.
You've got to stop coming around here
and calling, and standing so close
your breath on my neck.

Let's make a deal, I say, I'll bargain with you.
I'll be here. I'll do it. Just stop following me.
Stop watching me out of the corners
of your eyes from every doorway, car window,
across-the-room restaurant table.
How do I carry on?

I don't need you. I don't need you
to define me as woman, as vessel.

Wherever I go, there you are.
Look, we can work this out.
I'll give it up, I say. I won't fight.
My body you can take,
but the words are mine.

Swimming with Others

Sunday night, March in Miami, neon
spitting, casting shadows which run

at odd angles into alleyways. A man stands
pissing on a brick wall. We slide past, heads down,

hands shoved into pockets. Sunday night,
old men and women fanning under porch lights,

children splashing dirty puddles, legs bare
chattering into thick, silvery air.

Turning the corner, we pass through the barred door
of the all-night Cuban liquor store

where I buy cheap vodka to hide
under my shirt. Then quickly, we're inside

the Cameo Theater. The walls sweat
streaks which run from the ceiling; misty heat

and smoke rise from black
leather, mohawks, skull-painted jackets,

ripped jeans, steel-toed boots. Sunday night
near the stage, the air is electric, tight

as the fists raised to the first screeching
chords. Soon the pit becomes an undulating

school of bodies thrusting, shoving.
I watch from the edge, afraid to join,

until hands push from behind. I drown
in the gulp and dive of others. Down,

I fall into the pit and ride
back and forth, side to side.

The waves pull and swallow,
undertow and upside down I throw

my weight wholly. Holy water
down my back, my breasts.

Immersed, I am the slippery
skin of strangers.

Charity Bash

"It is very fashionable these days to speak of the poor;
unfortunately, it isn't fashionable to speak to them."

Mother Teresa

A long, slow zip up the back,
Black velvet over buttocks and hips,
We tease our hair and spritz our wrists.
We laugh and line our lips.

A smart bow tie and cummerbund,
The limo meets us at the door.
For fifty bucks we're at the gala
Getting wasted for the poor.

Near yards of cold cuts and petits fours,
Our friends wait at the old train station—
Beautiful people tanned all year long,
Just like their luggage from Louis Vitton.

Balloons, baguettes, and Polaroids—
We bump and grind across the floor.
In the smell of stale liquor and cigarettes,
We're getting wasted for the poor.

We brace ourselves against the stalls,
Tip the old woman at the door.
We're arm-in-arm on down the hall;
We got so wasted for the poor.

Next week at party number ten,
We'll wrap boxes for kids in the 'hood,
Not so sure if the gifts we've brought
Or the party makes us feel so good.

We're out of dresses, out of time.
We can't possibly give any more.
Besides, New Year's come and gone.
Yeah, we got wasted for the poor.

Hard Heat

We ride the slow, old elevator up
to the eighth floor. In the August air,
we try to speak with our hands,
my clipped Spanish, your answers
sí, sí when you finally understand.
You are washing dishes with the other
Mexicans. You need a health card.

Every month, your friends Felix, Manuel,
and Enrico mail their American *dolares* back
to Oaxaca and Ciudad de Mexico.
They haven't been home in years, polishing
the silver and wiping the toilets of tourists.
In the steamy spray of the dish pit,
your voices rise, ballads of love and loss.
For Manuel, the best news is Alaska—six months
on a boat, heaving and pitching in swells, to chip
salty ice from the bow, pull steaming
nets up to the deck, the silver salmon
shimmering like coins.

Back in the elevator, the slow passage of flights,
floor lights flash through door cracks
as we climb higher. On six, three more crowd on:
someone who looks like a lawyer, a woman
in a blue suit, a uniformed man. We all squeeze
together, but you flatten against the rear wall

as we shudder on up again. Your eyes narrow—
a dark animal, invisible. I know the man
to be a park ranger—someone who drags
a deer carcass from the side of the road, digs
a hole, drops the body in a fading light.
But the shiny badge and cornered hat—
you imagine he notices your jeans from Penney's,
Converse hi-tops and thinks them strange.
You hold your breath, your chest unmoving as if
a simple exhalation would rush out in Spanish.
Then the man could turn, his own eyes narrowing
to cuff your alien wrists, send you back to the drawn out
dust of the border which settles softly in hard heat.

La policia. Sometimes at night you wake, your toes
ablaze, your feet aflame, where other prisoners
have woven tissue in between each digit, lit the ignitable
fibers. They hide, secretly watching your lashes flutter,
until you rise up, screaming, stamping out the fire.

Before the Sentencing

I won't say the prison yard sunsets
were more beautiful than others,
their fiery expanse spread out
over the Palouse, the science of air
pollution more intense, burning
just outside the razor wire. I won't say
the men stood around in clumps
as I walked past, the distinct smell
of industrial disinfectant, bleach and
the blackest of sweats. I won't say
the light cast a kind of peace over
the trimmed grass, the austere, lonely
buildings. Because I won't imagine you
there, some other woman come to read
poetry, walking past you in the yard,
into the burning evening, her lavender
smell like clean laundry, like something
you'll try to forget.

Oh, moon, oh, orange, orange moon rising
behind the powerlines and beyond the fields
of green winter wheat, and beyond tomorrow,
your face before me, black half-moons under
your eyes, moons of our fingers pressed together
across the bullet proof glass, moon of a long
summer without you; oh, love, orange moon
rising, the ironic sunset, the door's

click-clack behind me. The walk to the car. The long, long drive by moonlight, by darkness, in silence.

Cinco de Mayo

My heels click down the dark
black stairwell past the back
entrance to the parking garage.
Late, impatient, I go alone,
not waiting for Tom or Keith
to walk me out. I round the corner
where four shadowy figures stand
silently. In the night's uncommon warmth
and stillness, their brown eyes
follow my hips as I pass. *Hola, princesa!*
¿Dondé vas? You look nice tonight.
Half-smiling, I continue to my car.
One, with skin like polished walnut,
taunts me, *Oh, nióa de mis sueóos,*
we sing you a song before you go?
As they follow me, I'm fumbling
with my keys. Suddenly,

their voices bloom
into harmony. Fingers snapping
keep rhythm as the notes grow
like trailing ivy. Building, the sound winds
around a blue Mazda and a broken Ford,
through my hair, wrapping my ankles.
The music fills the exhausted air, resonates
off the low ceilings and cement pilings
holding offices, an art gallery,

the restaurant where I'd worked
all night. If I could, I'd remain
here: a statue covered
with ivy and blooming notes.

Psyche Visits Young Pablo

> *Salud, amor, salud por todo*
> *lo que cae y lo que florece.*
> —Neruda

I
I watch him sleep, dark
and sweet on the threshing floor
a bed of yellow straw.

I slip to his side,
know he will not cry out,
take my pleasure in the night.

I smell dust of day, taste
sweat of golden fields,
slide palms across smooth chest,
leave before light.

II
In the musk of yellow straw
amid oats, barley, I sleep
in rhythms of others' snores.

Awakened by simple stirring,
the closeness of another's breath,
a warm mouth to mine.

Her full hips rise beneath
the pressure of my palms. I think
of morning, golden like wheat:
the fields on the road to Santiago.

III
Golden morning, he rises
alone. But there are too many
with black braids dividing strong backs.

All day he searches to find dark eyes,
follows full hips to find
the familiar curve of night.

All day the wheat ripples,
rustles like close whispers,
cut by the arcing scythes
and the interruption of dream.

This is How I Tell You, *mi amiga*

I close the door behind me.
The dark hallway, tiled floors,
walls stuccoed quiet and open
to the courtyard. I can't remember
which way we'd come up. Even now,
as I say this, I hold my breath.

All I hear are my shoes, frightened
on stone steps worn smooth, dipped
in the center. Six a.m. the only people
in the lobby are the desk clerk
and another man mopping. They say nothing
to me: *Americana. Los ojos azules.*
Ella no habla espanol.

Only hours earlier we rode the open-air cab
through the sticky night along the water's edge,
past the neon tourist bars to the old city
where the Belmar sits on the sand
facing west. I waited in a marble entryway
lined with heavy wooden rockers.
Even inside, the singular sound was waves
rolling onto rocks. We didn't speak.

80,000 pesos for a room down dim
hallways. Dank and grim, Room 524
has no towels. The ceiling fan

hangs broken and motionless, a stifled wish
above the bed. On the balcony wrapped
in bedspreads, we sit and smoke, his careful
English curling above my head.

Each way I look, white and pink
squared buildings chiseled
into cliffs above the churning surf.
This hotel, once elegant, now
the only sounds: our lowered voices,

the sloshing of mop water
across the chipped tile floor.
The clerk is kind and dials The Playa where you
answer, your voice thick with sleep.

These particular sounds surround me
as I stand holding the receiver
deciding if I should speak
across the lines looped pole to pole,
black against this day
we are to leave.

Upstairs, the heat of morning
mists through slatted windows
and open balcony door.

Soon, he may forget fractured frost on windows,
a sudden flash of daffodil on roadsides, the curve
of his lover's shoulders, then hips striped
by light through Venetian blinds. If only he could forget
clear typed print upon a page, lines to love and follow
So much depends on summer, gardens
of tomatoes warm and dusty with dirt.

Instead he wants to touch light beyond
his eyes: the absolute velvet of her skin beneath
his own hips, the pungent steam of bread rising,
the suckling lip of an orange. No more
the various cumulus: just the musical way
of rain water. This surrounds him:
a dark map of sounds he takes inside
when words rise to his fingertips.

Circles

Late October, we drove the brown, ribboned
hills north of Reardon and Davenport
to the orchards. The apples and pears
have ripened, you said, the sun is shining.

We turned the truck up any old driveway,
hollered, and someone would wander out
to show their bins of fruit. Or better, cider.
We stood by while the farmer and his son

tumbled apples down the chute, set up
the presser, turned on the giant machine.
A deafening noise, rumbling vibrations
produced a thin, brown stream we gulped

from paper cups. I bought a gallon from the wife
in a flowered smock, trying to divert her
from your story: a novel set in an orchard,
whether she'd be open to research.

I pictured you sitting late at the farmer's
Summer table, your steno pad filled with scribbles,
steamy plates of vegetables, ripe tomatoes,
the whole family leaning into your words.

For two years, you had spoken of your wife:
her perfect ordering of silver in wooden drawers,

the way her apron caked with flour after baking,
the long cold of Saskatchewan in her fingers.

You papered your office walls with crayoned
pictures, Dante's seven levels, a brooding crucifix
beside the window light late on Friday evenings.
Not long after, you stood obsessed in a rondelle

of circling crows, blackbirds borrowed
from Stevens, another woman whose ankles
drove you mad. Your wife knew nothing,
eight hours away, of the gypsy women

before her, the detective-actor life you led.
We watched you—your friends who fed you
pasta, listened to various versions of the same
story, let you get away with small discrepancies.

Where could this end? We were writers, too, hooked
on plot development, your small drama unfolding.

We walked the long orchard rows, the Bosc
and Bartlett's perfume thick between us.
Bees drunk on the downfall of heavy limbs.
Through humming autumn light and tears,

you told me she no longer loved you.
By this time, I wasn't sure who *she* was.
I'm bound to her by duty, you said.
My boys are in good hands.

But what about love? I wanted to know,
in the orchard's darkening shadows, the crows,
the drunken bees circling the fallen fruit.

Blue Waves of Light

Oddly glorious, this blending of dusk,
moist and golden summer heat. Shadows
soften leaves of oak and poplar,
music thick with crickets. The clink-clank
of a tin fork inside his lunch pail marks the weight
of steps walking. Boots press into black dirt
rutted from lumbering trucks of coal.
In the hills, dense and emerald,
throaty frogs call and mosquitoes hum
to the occasional flash of lightning bug
which hangs in the heavy air. Appalachian hillsides
of wild flowers, dogwood, goldenrod grow soft
beside uneven edges of Rowan County
twisting through Olive Hill and Sandy Hook.

Every so often he coughs, spits black.
Black creases his eyes, rims his nostrils,
ears, fills every fold of his face.
Black tattooed his pores.
He walks and walks

up the hill. His crooked back throbs from bending,
stretching, pulling the sooty rock from the vein.
This is all he knows. Any other world may exist
only in the glow from the windows as he walks
up the worn steps of his home.
Each step creaks as he sees his children

and wife tangled on the springless couch.
Screen door is open. Flies buzz
to the droning television
where under the blue light,
they are transfixed.

Enough

I
Sometimes I lie half awake
for an hour until I can no longer
bear it, wrench myself from bed
at 2 a.m., stumble downstairs
to fill the tub as the blood seeps.
I immerse and imagine I'd never
be good at babies, couldn't stand
the pain, even if it meant some life
would come of it. I examine my life
with him, who watched five births,
and I think mothering his should be
enough. I float waiting for my womb
to stop its fluttering and give me
some peace. Some sleep.
A quiet heart beating.

II
We light candles and place our hands
on her oiled belly. We tell her
she will be strong, a good mother.
The women around the circle talk
vaginal and cesarean, their eyes glaze
as they recollect. There are two of us
whose wombs don't remember anything
except the waves that wake us.
We press our palms again, feel
the baby's pulse under our fingertips.

All Life Leads to Suffering

for the children of Sri Ram Ashram

Babaji watches the children
who walk to him as he reaches
in his bag. They know who he is.
He never speaks, but his eyes shine
clear, and warm. I can barely
meet them, though I want to.
He knows the children will grow,
join the world of grapple and grasp.
He knows it is futile, inevitable. But
he smiles at them, gives them all
a stick of candy, a sweet
to touch their tongues when later
they remember the presence of God.

What Children Hear

how sweet the sound that saved a wretch like me . . .
                                                Amazing Grace

In South Bronx, Cliffie takes Jonathan
on an extra special tour. He munches
Oreos from a baggie while he points
to various places of interest.
His other hand holds tight
to Jonathan, a man he just met.
They pass the needle exchange
where stuffed bears hang
from a dying oak, a place for children
to play while their parents make the trade.
"I saw a boy shot in the head
right over there . . . they burn bodies."
He shows puffing stacks
of incinerated medical waste. He frees
his hand to reveal an inhaler— a visual
aide. Cliffie waves to people as they pass:
she's got no place. His brother's doin' time.

They walk the whole of Jackson Ave.
careful to cross over the street
where cousins sit with nothin'
but time, arriving finally at St. Ann's,
where Cliffie lets go

His job's finished.
He wants to know when
Jonathan will be back. He says
there's more to see.

A Long Time After Vietnam

My first Christmas home I asked him,
my college vocabulary like a mouthful
of pebbles saying: nuclear capability.

Just suppose as we drove icy December
back roads, I thought of how we never locked
our doors when he was home, his boots echoing
down wooden hallways, he'd pause
before my mother's room, then enter.

Just suppose, I didn't think of planes like flocks of geese
gone wrong, a button pushed, decades undone.
But then the question hung there, tentative as ice.
"What is it," his hands grown cold, gripping
the wheel, "that you think I do?"

Just Before the Father Left

My sister Melissa is luminous.
Her baby a perfect little buddha,
all belly, blissful—anyone can love her.

My little tomboy sister
who refused to wear a shirt,
her blonde hair in ringlets,
shoulder to shoulder
with neighborhood boys.

Now she's milk-heavy
and mothersome.
She sleeps lightly, listening for
the baby's breath, its even
measured sweetness. She rises
to watch through white bars
under the tinkling mobile—
anyone can love her.

Bath-time ritual, a round
cherub, fat mermaid. My sister
sings Under the Sea,
dumps water over the bald head,
sputtering laughter.
My sister is perfect
at this. I'm not surprised,
anyone can love her.

Anuradha's Ride to the Ganga

Mahadeva Jaya Jaya Tripurari
Shiva Shankar Jaya Gangadhari
Gangadhari, Gangadhari
Shiva Shankar Jaya Gangadhari!

The orphans are knobby knees,
elbows, and white teeth;
their voices rise high, high
for the holy water,
the sacred river.
One dip, one tiny sip
will wash away suffering
and loneliness.

The wagon sways
over the rutted road.
They sing louder,
louder to conjure
Shiva,
destroyer and creator
at once.

Holy, holy water!
They offer themselves up
to the dream of it.

Becoming Santa

The night before, I followed my mother
quietly through the house, padding
after her in my footsie p.j.'s. We made
several trips to the garage and back,
to place unwrapped presents
under the tree. Someone got a Baby
Tenderlove, a trike, a record album.

Instead of snow men in the front yard,
carrot nose and all that, we had
California, Vietnam, and Watergate.
Mrs. Major, we called my mom
after Dad got promoted overseas
and we baked her a cake.

When she'd leave the house, I'd hide
from the blonde-haired babysitter
and sneak back to my father's side
of the closet. I'd wrap myself in the blue
velour of his robe, breathing his smell,
remembering the sound of the Sunbeam
as it turned the corner, no muffler,
squeaking brakes: Daddy's home!

In the photo, my mother is younger
than I am now— barely thirty, wrinkle-free.
My sisters wear red flannel nighties,

their soft baby-hair in ringlets, tiny teeth
bared to the camera. Off to the side,
I'm chewing Christmas candies, my mouth
contorted, my eyes scrunched shut.
I look suspicious, as if I had been let in
on something I couldn't give back.

You don't think I can imagine
what this feels like. I can't imagine wind
tearing your eyes, the sustained moment
of a trick. Now it's ollie, nollie, grinding,
waxing, sliding, defying the gravity
of this time in your life. I can't imagine
subtle balance up on your toes,
rock back on your heels, the grip tape's
sandpaper grab on your shoe bottoms,
the metallic slide on a handrail, the up-and-over
the ramp. *This is freedom*, you think,
nothing can stop me now.
Not bloody bails on the sidewalk,
not cops cruising the parking lots,
not teachers or principals
or parents, who know nothing
about being fourteen and free.

Even though I don't understand,
you ask me to watch the skate video
anyway, and there he is: Baryshnikov
at Venice Beach. He drags the toe
of the board along asphalt; he executes
the grand jeté over the staircase; he twirls and swirls
around and around, front trucks like satin slippers.
His angular arms curve in first position. He dances.
I get it. I'm listening, but you can't imagine,

and I don't know how to tell you
there will be more dancing, this flight
of your definite body. There will be more.

Panic That Sets In

Steam rises from the kitchen sink.
A boy in black rubber boots and straw hat
wades toward the peninsula sunset
through the timothy and other grasses,
which brush his hips and shoulders
sometimes. He's lied to me,
so I've bought him the plant food
he carries in a white bucket
to treat imaginary bamboo
he's growing out beyond
the wooded property line.

Later after he's gone to bed,
I'll carry the flashlight out,
stealthy and black,
to the spindly *Cannabis* leaves
and tug their young stems,
pull them up
by the roots.
It isn't because I've never
liked the sweet smoky smell,
or the musty taste rolling
down my throat and holding
there. The silliness
that is inevitable.

But I've seen it

on the faces of the others
the panic that sets in
when they recognize
years unfolding
before them. *This*
is just a small thing:
the white roots like bones
under lamplight.

Daytime Shatters Loose

for the women who wait

It is wartime, so I don't know
if any of what I think or feel is real.
I just sit here with the warm
back porch step beneath me, an ember
loosely balanced between my fingers
and I suck in. Suck in the lemon-
laden air, look up at a simple sliver
of moon. On any other night, I might
think you look at the same moon, but you
are hemispheres away, and the sun burns
into your atmosphere like lemons. So many
lemons we can't squeeze them all.
Can't make lemonade. Can't buy enough
bags of sugar to sweeten them.

Mornings I tightly braid our daughters' hair.
Left, then right, then left. I try to weave
all their curls into plaits which daytime shatters
loose. One names her dog after you; one dances
to California Dreamin' in her room; and one sings
Bah, bah black sheep, have you any wool?
The purest voice I know travels reel to reel,
then back again. There's a wavering
ocean I hear in your voice as you tell the girls

you're under a tree waiting
for a coconut to fall on your head.
It's the least of my worries, now.

I imagine you know the layout here:
the way the constant summer air shifts
unnaturally from room to room,
the matted green of a rented carpet,
the jarring of periodic quakes.
I imagine the room you don't have
with your back to the windshield,
four other men in a cockpit the size
of a bathroom. The rumbling cavern
beneath you is three times the size
of this house. What's the percentage of bomb
to man? The ratio of waking
to sleeping? Of seconds to lifetimes?

Some days I think scrubbing the floor
will make a difference (like the rolling
of bandages or scraps of tin foil).
On my hands and knees, I watch the wrench
of raw knuckles as I swipe left, then right.
It isn't just that letters take weeks
and phone calls are few, but it won't be
your voice or your block-lettered hand,
but a uniform, a telegram, a lie.

I play bridge with another wife.
We make halter tops and white slacks

to meet the POWs at the flight line.
We smoke, turn thirty, take our kids to the beach.
Camp along Ventura highway. In the rain,
the girls run out to the sidewalks,
search the ivy for snails,
follow their opaline trails.
This isn't even a letter, love.
It's a night of lemon, a sliver
of moon crook'd in the corner
of a thick black sky.

Her Misery

Isn't he merciful
to stand on the edge of the ditch,
his blue body taut, October
light filtering through big leaf
maples and madrones, rifle snugged in
at his shoulder?

She's crouched down in moss
and salal, the dark branches
a cave closing around her.
She sees him out there
in the light, the sun
splintering off the metal star
pinned to his heart. Her eyes
wide, she trembles, the blood
already welling.

Isn't he merciful? The onlookers
exclaim at the side of the road,
cars humming past, death bedding
down in the trees. Put her out,
they think, of her misery.

She waits, watches as if she's passing
by in a car, strains to hear the shot.

Like This, Like That

What I remember is the pink scar
along his cheekbone, his hair sandy
and thick, his mouth wet and soft—
Buddy Stone, whose name follows me
into the dark back seats of my remembering.
My body hovering a little above us
there, its quick and furious happening,
no I'd said, then the slow, dull ache. No.
I watched myself glide through polished
hallways, bells ringing, ringing past
heavy oak doors, rectangular windows
I could peer in, to get a glimpse of him,
the one I'd given it up for, the one
who never spoke to me again.

I remember in the days after, standing
in the drafty warehouse between flatbeds
stuffing tissue paper onto Homecoming floats,
the tennis coach's look of recognition.
What I don't remember is how he said
he'd show me the right way. The right way,
I remember his smirk and his cool,
sweaty hands. I can't tell you why
I followed him. I can't tell you what
made me watch him methodically assembling
cushions in the back of a van, my climbing in
and what followed. I only know I wanted

to do it the right way.
I wanted to know what it took
to change someone's life forever,
taking them in like that.

Where does she go? That girl whose fingers
were just here, just now pressing their round
moons into your back. *This is it?* I remember
thinking *this is my destiny?* To lie back
like this? I can't tell more
about the undoing

Dancing with My Dad on a Rented Dance Floor,

I came out. At the Ladies' Auxiliary earlier that week,
we girls had covered old cigar boxes with flowered fabric
and scraps of lace. To collect donations at the dance,
we'd pass between tables offering potted centerpieces,
garish carnations and ferns, to the highest bidder.

On the edge of the golf course, under looming cottonwood,
I stood stiffly, dressed in white, waiting with my father,
my warm hand held aloft in his white glove.

I strained to see over his shoulder, beyond the glow
of the striped tent to the slender flashlight beams
of the valets. Young men in jeans and white shirts,
who parked cars for country club members.
We weren't members, but any debutante would do.

Beyond the backdrop of cicadas and violins,
I met eyes searching through the vague cigarette haze.
And for that instant, I knew the figure-eight's of twirling
hoop skirts and taffeta hadn't crossed me over,
made me fit to be a *wife.* Nor my name announced
clearly, decidedly, by the chairman of the ball.
There was something else out there,
in the wide and generous night.

Perfectly

Geneva, 1979

Those streets the cleanest I'd ever seen—
not a crumb, a butt, a crumpled paper.
Along the water's edge, the fountain's spray
arced against robin-egg blue and spattered
clear and fresh, blown by the wind to my skin,
and held there, like cold tears. A lovely place.
A perfectly manicured city: lined streets
with shops of chocolates and clocks.
Crisp men in suits on corners.

At sixteen, longing for something
like love, years from the sadness
of quick rivers, smudged windows, burnt fields,
the obscure fog of chance, *yes*; chance, *no.*
There was no reason for me to stand,
holding the rail at the Alp-fed lake as if
I might fall. As if I might bloody up
the street with my simple American
sadness, my anonymous face, my place
in a crowd of tourists, gripping the cool
metal of winter. And water. Bruises
of water, perfect circular drops blown
flawless by gray wind to color my clothes
a bit darker. *What is it? What is it?*
In that lake where I won't feel the bottom?

Girls Games

You run down
the waxed court
a little shy,
a little excited
because the ball
could be yours, next.
Your hair's worked
its flyaway out
of the plastic barrette;
you're all caught up
in the bounce and dribble.
You and other fourth graders
run in a bunch.
Your coach yells
Spread out!
Arms up!

During time-out,
the older girl referees
stand one-hand
on their hips, twirling
their slick, green whistles
around and around,
the black and white
of their shirts important.
They will show you
the way to catch a ball

and pass. The way
to hold your body
for your first kiss,
your mouth wet
and sweet. But this comes
later. Today, their pony tails
swish and bob
with their heads
as they wait
for the signal to play.

Finally, the ball
floats to you
like a great, orange
balloon. You grab it
like that, and run.
The shrill whistle
yells *traveling!*
A striped girl
takes you aside,
her hand so soft
on your shoulder,
and quietly
tells you
the rules.

What Eliza Tells Her Daughter While Putting Up Tobacco

I don't think bad boys have changed much
since I was young. Bad boys change
as they grow older, but they're basically
the same when they're young. Bad boys
are delicious, but you don't want to marry
them. It's even better if you never fall
for one, but you will. It's something
some girls just go through. Sad thing,
some girls don't pass on through,
they just get one bad boy
after another.

Some bad boys'll tell you they love you
right away. One, for example, said
"I love you more'n yer momma does."
This was a dead giveaway because
he didn't know my momma at all. She's
the kind who stands at the back door
in her apron yelling, "Yoo-hoo! Time
for Supper!" She's the kind
who stops whatever she's doing
to give that boy a *don't forget*
you've got the most precious cargo speech
so that by the time you leave,
you know this is the last time
he'll ever come to the door again.

From here on out, it's dutch treat,
meet me at Frisch's Big Boy parking lot.

You're not listening, I can tell. I can see
by the way you're not looking up,
your hair curling around your
sweaty neck, out here in the sun.
You're thinking I don't know, just because
I'm older. Is there nothin' I can say?
I suppose I could start on the Bible.
The old *hold an aspirin*
between your knees,
sin, and all that.

When bad boys get older, they get bold.
They'll follow you around like dogs, sniffing
at your haunches, and they go after you
into the Ladies'. Some'll just walk right on in,
like they always sit down to pee,
just to see how far you will let them go.
You should act like they're crazy
because they are.

Most bad boys have mothers, but these women
don't know what to do with them either.
Some just stop askin' whereabouts.
It's no use to ask after them
at the bootlegger's. You know
they been there. You can smell
that booze as soon as you see 'em

smiling at you, sauntering over
the way they do. The next thing you know,
you've steamed up the back seat
of an old Cordova, and you can't,
for the life of you, remember how you
got there. This is the way bad boys are: smooth
as silk. They smell like leather and sweat
and cigarettes, which don't taste so bad,
at first.

Fairy Tale Girl Gets Married

Fairy Tale Girl graduates
summa cum laude
from the U K or U Dub.
Doesn't matter, she's
done it. All her sisters
squeal, her Big Bro grunts
and snorts. *You go, Girl!*
Fairy Tale Girl is pinned
and engaged and defrocked
in the passive tense.
Fairy Tale Girl buys
a white dress anyway.
The other Delta Meltas
wear lavender,
their manicured fingers
tap-tapping on the bar
for another round.
Fairy Tale Girl's wedding
cake is purple and green.
The reception is the scene
for which frat parties
were practice. Next day,
Fairy Tale fights
with her new husband.
He's drunk and throws
the rented punch bowl
across the room at her.

Game over. Outside,
across the street,
the young Mexicans
stand in the grass smoking.
They watch Fairy on the stoop
from the corners of their black,
black eyes. The thump
of salsa from the radio
the pulse inside a bloody lip.

What We Do

I'm sure it was funny to the women in purple smocks
whose purpose was to tell us how to behave
at your night wedding in the Cathedral
of St. John the Evangelist. Funny
because I was dressed *to the nines*—
slim teal, high heels, and down on my knees
pulling the layers of tulle and lace up over my head,
foraging for your undergarments. It was more
than bridesmaid protocol: checking your teeth
for lipstick, spraying your hair in place. It's what we do
for each other, sister, when it's 102 degrees outside,
and your merry widow's creeping up, its satin flower
rising above the neckline of your dress, and I'm down
there
for the third or fourth yank of the night.

Like June, some years later, you'll stand in the kitchen
I'm leaving, lining boxes with newspaper, stacking plates
and candles, cookbooks from Mom. You'll know when
to stop what you're doing, the cupboards swung open,
our father loading chairs in the blue truck outside.
You'll know to touch my shoulder, then, because I won't
answer your questions: which pots to take, which ones to
leave.

First, big shovel-fulls,
the cool metal
slicing down hard
through orange clay
and underneath
the turning over
of gray rocks
grown ancient
against gnarled roots.
Determined,
she's on her knees,
her hands grip
a hoe, small
miner's pick
she raises
above her head
like surrender to sever
hidden roots, their white
foam blood
on her fingers.
In her hair,
the messy knots
of memory. Debris
rises, a small mountain
beside her work.
She's on her belly
now, reaching in,

clawing, sifting,
pulling apart
looser loam,
tiny pebbles,
hairy roots.
She climbs down
into grief's dark
rectangle, her body
a tuber to harden
over winter,
maybe rise
in spring.

What She Said

Blue Mary stands to the left
of the altar. Her arms are open,
palms slightly raised. She can't
move from her place no matter
the number of candles aflame
at her feet. She's here
because she said *yes*. *Yes*
to holiness, to God,
to light. She opened up
like a lotus, unblinking love.

Blue Mary's lips are wooden,
her eyes half-closed. First,
she said yes, then bowed
her head. Said *yes*
to the dust in her mouth
the day her heart breaks,
the word choked back in her throat.

From the Waitress Journals

I. Ladies Lunch

Well, I did have that little salad
before. You know, the one with the walnuts
and the blue cheese?

Yes, but Mary had two martinis.
Stoli. That had to be pretty expensive.

Well, mine's $8.48 exactly,
plus tax. Let's see, what's 8.2 percent of $8.48?

Don't forget the tip. My Jack, now he says *no more
than ten percent;* it's just a crime how much
everything costs these days!

Oh, I forgot coffee. How much is coffee?
Damn, I've got to add that to my part.

This is ridiculous, I tell you.

Just let me find my calculator.
It's somewhere in my purse.

I only had ice water—I'm not paying for Mary's martinis.

If each of us could've just remembered what she ordered

and kept track, we wouldn't be wasting all this time.

Here, *here.* Let's see if the waitress
could just bring us another menu?

Miss? Oh, Miss?

II. Nightmare: Tables Sit for Hours One Fourth of July

You're on top of me
pushing and pushing
and I have this waitress fantasy:
we've pulled two tables together,
fucking in the middle of the dining room
amid the silverware and plastic menus.
In my section, customers ask for bowls
of soup, glasses of wine. "Miss?
Miss?" but I can't get up
from this incessant bumping
my head against the marble table,
pounding, your face twisted
into a grimace of what's supposed to be
delight. I say, "Just a minute.
Just a minute! I'll be right with you . . ."
I'm ruining my chances
for tips from these people,
so you leave me
a couple of bucks
under the salt shaker when you go.

III. Green Dye in the Chicago River

I'm not sure how it happened,
but here I am doing what I swore I never would.
It's St. Patrick's, and I'm working O'Reilly's
piano lounge, wearing a green plastic hat
and a black skirt cut up to *here*
sloshing out green beers and two-dollar
Irish Coffees. If I smell another Bushmill's—
and stop it, I mean stop! Not another flush-faced
middle-aged suit without a drop o' blarney
to tug on my arm, my blouse, my ass—what's the matter
with you people? Something in the water?

IV. Blair Elementary End-of-the-Year Luncheon

Really, I have done something with myself
since fourth grade. I swear. I'm in graduate school
now, something useful: English.
I adjust the bow tie and black vest, pour
a little more wine. The old librarian
still looks the same, even though I'm twenty
years older, careful not to catch my hair on fire
after I toss the 151 over the prime rib, light it,
carry its blue flames through the door
on a silver tray. I try real hard not to screw up
the cherries jubilee (also flaming)
when I set the match to it, watch the sugar
sparkle and pop. I'm ten again, or twenty-one.
It's seven a.m. on Saturday when the phone rings
after I cocktailed all night, walking

the damp streets to my apartment, carrying
too much cash to be safe. It's my mother's voice,
again, *what are you doing with your life?*

V. Seattle's First Raw Bar

Oysters are an aphrodisiac, Stu says
as I roll my eyes and consider the slimy,
gray animal poised on a saltine, my first oyster
and only blind date. I remember this
as John from Puget Sound Shellfish Company
is showing the Raw Bar servers
the fresh Penn Cove Selects,
Hamma Hammas and Westcott Bays.
He's wearing a tough rubber glove,
prying the curved knife between
the clamped shells, telling us to *be careful,
one slip and you'll cut the palm
of your hand.* I knew a line cook
who'd done this— fourteen stitches
in the fleshy cushion between his thumb
and forefinger. *Shucking is an art*, John's saying,
as we watch him deftly slide the shells apart,
slurp up the salty juices, swallow
the tender shellfish in a gulp.

VI. Bus Station Blues

Be careful in there,
where they fold the napkins,
stack the silver, away from

the diners' eyes, the manager's
glare. You can come around
the corner loaded up
with plates and glasses
to find someone eating
out of the bus tubs, or buying a nickel
bag. Or one time, two gay
waiters, one to the other,
"I'll never balk at mini-pads
again," the short one says,
"my balls have been dry all week!"

VII. Kitchen Dates: A How To

Chefs can be somewhat hazardous.
They've always got that big roll-up
of knives. They think they're so smart
in their checked pants, starched white
coats, tall paper hats, their hands scarred
from the grill, burners left on too long.
You can get their attention: *Order please?*
One short ring of the bell. Smile sweetly.

The good ones will cook for you.
They know it's more than a job—
the preparation of food. Seduction is
showing up at the door with a cooler full
of exotic olives, pate, polenta con gorgonzola.
This is foreplay. Don't get in the way.
It's better just to watch their quick hands,
the uniformity of onions and garlic.

Always make the appropriate noises
when they raise the spoon to your lips.
Blow a little. Widen your eyes.
Make that sound that comes from
the back of your throat.

VIII. Trips to the Walk-in

I'm hooked. I'm high. I'm screaming down I-75
in a black Datsun 280Z with my legs wrapped
around the waist of someone gorgeous
as he tries to drive in the right hand lane.
I'm sneaking inside an office building after hours,
to swipe the pictures, pencils, ink blotter
from the desk to feel the cold mahogany
on my backside in the dark. I'm every clandestine
rendezvous, every trip to the walk-in
or out back near the recycle barrels,
the glass sorted into clear, brown, and green.
I'm wiping smeared lipstick on the underside
of my white apron only to appear at your table,
may I take your order please? What will you have tonight?
I'm standing there flushed and smiling,
so serious about Insalata Mista and
Cappelini D'Angelo. I'm open, a raw nerve, bare
shoulders pressed up against the craggy bark
of a Douglas fir. I'm hazy eyed, long after
closing time, and last call, where under the table
I've run my bare toes up along side his leg.
My face is set, flawless. Unmoved. There is nothing
subtle about what I want. Nothing virtuous.

Nothing. No one knows. No one can tell
from my face. I'm gone. I've lost it.
What if I never go back?

IX. Guest First (A Corporate Love Song)

The hostess knows best
how to think *fuck you,*
and smile at the same time.
People will tell her anything
to get what they want.
They must have a window,
their mother's here from dusty
Oklahoma, and they need a water view.
It's her job to put their needs
before hers, but she knows exactly
when to lock eyes, when to
lean in a little as if she's giving them
some special treatment
sending them to the bar for an hour.
She gets paid to tell them how happy
she is to see them, to ask their names,
and remember them. *Let me check
on that,* she'll say as she leaves them
at the desk. *Oh, yes, delightful!*
They may choose a quaint table
somewhat near the kitchen, or,
(she'll pause here to look
at her wrist), perhaps enjoy a drink
in the bar? They are, after all,
guests for dinner.

X. Ten Minute Breaks

Out back, Sam and Joe looked for a poem
in the oily green dumpster behind Kell's.
Seattle was small, my life smaller.
For the third time that week,
I watched them from the stoop,
wiping my hands on a cotton bar towel.
A heavy grayness hung limp around downtown,
little rivers of last night's Guinness and Harp
slid along Post Alley past their digging
down to the murky pool of the Market.

In no time at all, I was far
from the rustling skirt of the city.
I left the last chunks of chowder
in the bottom of my chipped cup,
my blue Mazda with the ripped front seat
and the coffee-stained carpet,
the parking lot of the Hungry Bear Café.
I slipped into the bare trees just up the road
from Hamma Hamma on Hood Canal.
I walked toward angles of darkness,
mossy silence so loud
I wanted to swallow it
whole.

Strange Bruises

It seems like weeks, now.
My body, a foreign land
I visit but barely remember.
The odd tastes and smells
of another city, another culture.
What country have we inhabited?
I trace blue lines along
hip bones or shins, forearms,
and the small knobs of sacrum—
stopover spots, rest areas,
where bruises fade
to mauve and yellow,
to the slow purpling ache.

Because

> *There is nothing one man will not do to another.*
> Carolyn Forché

Because upstairs, the leggy dance girls
with their perfect breasts prepared for the night—
Sierra, Nadia, Alexis—their stage names like tassels
adhered to nipples and fringed thongs. Because
downstairs the husband waited on the couch
by the t.v. while in the next room his wife
eased her hips down over the paraplegic's costly
mouth. Because tomorrow your mother might be
adjusting the seams of fishnet stockings
in the tavern ladies' room, her date dark
beside you at the bar. When you turn to me,
finally, in my bed, in wonder and suspicion,
I hold you anyway, with everything I've got
to give you, finite and loving as it is.

Trying to Speak: A Dream Sequence

Dream I—Lights

We move through dappled paths
out onto a meadow in dawn
where red morning sky waits
impatiently behind cragged silhouettes.
We look down at our feet
cracked and callused with walking
through so many lives,
and we long for cool dew relief
of timothy now wet and frosty
in autumn's brilliant sadness.

We have been to this meadow before,
to lie on a sedge bed where fawns born
of mothers like our own have lain.
We lay there a long while
watching the sky change, the light
warming in mid-day, steam rising
from loam and moving across a violet later,
sinking cool, then cold, into black,
lit by a half-moon. Each star
we long for knowing
the points of pain a body
will have in this world.

We leave the meadow, walk back
through the stippled path worn smooth
from infinite feet. And we hold on,
hold on to each other as we walk headstrong
into the pulsing light of night, neon, thump.

It could have been drums, lights' glow
from city streets with cars and people
turning away from each other
looking for points of pain under needles,
the backs of hands, words like slaps.
The stars are lost to the strobes
and aching spotlights circling the night sky.

Dream II— Stories

Yes, I hold your head in my hands.
I examine you closely. I tell you what
I see, how the scars, folds, wrinkles
tell their own stories. Where you've been.
Who you've been before me. Your head
is so heavy in my hands. It weighs as much
as a life. I peer into the swirling black
of your pupil, the infinite iris. I read.
I can't go any deeper than this.

Dream III— Voices

You watch me from the small audience.
I speak your life to strangers,
people you wouldn't share your bed with,

but now you do because I'm telling it that way.
I'm narrating and painting and flourishing
and embellishing. I've stolen your story,
your words, your dirtiness and suffering.
You try to explain from your chair, which is soft
and comfortable gone cold. You've lost
your voice. Now you know everyone
is looking at you. They are wondering if
you are the one in the poem.

Dream IV— Words

We're trying to speak to one another
in a large room, surrounded by the din
of others. It's a party, where no one has fun,
their features exaggerated caricatures.
Malnourished bodies connected to enormous noses
and mouths. I try to whisper
in your ear. We should yell, our
words flung out across thick air,
but we don't, we whisper instead.

Dream V— Ashes

I go downstairs to the wood stove
still burning, the coals like Clifton's rubies
in "Fury." I write the dreams
on a piece of paper and put it
into the fire. The edges of the dreams
curl up on themselves, the words distort,
like words from real dreams, but I can't

pick them out, they're in there,
beginning to smoke and turn black.
I let them go. I said them.
What do you want from me?
I say to the fire. *I can't hear you.*
What do you want?

Retrograde

Nothing works. The faucet
drips. The one I love
won't stay away from
drink. I'm full
of pity, fat words
which make no sense.
What I need
directly: something
to sink into
a cool blue
sense that all
is
in its place.

Loaded

The air cracks wide open. After a small deafening,
it echoes back and forth across the tree-lined valley.

Smells like caps we popped on the sidewalk with rocks,
but bigger and more silent later. Fades back into breath,

a throat cleared, the click-clack of the reload.

What surprised me the most was that it wasn't at all
what I'd expected. It wasn't death in my hands.

Call it 12, 16, or 20 gauge shotgun, the slap of butt
under my arm, the softest spot to bruise. It wasn't my life,

heavy in my hands, hot metal, but revolvers—22, 32,
357 Magnum. Adding the numbers, so I could stand there empty

shells scattered around my feet, red and black. I wasn't sexy
at all, just me, dangerous inside myself, firing round after round.

What I found I wanted was to be accurate. To be right on
the mark. To shoot dead center, the glass busting out

in rainbowed splinters clear, brown, green, the late light
slipping behind the hills. I wanted to cock it. Pull it. Hit it.

Whatever it was just outside me there.

Dissolved

Never ask the question you won't
answer. Like what about the woman
with the toaster beside you, holding
a frayed cord like a tassel, and the couple
before the judge whose trees were cut
for someone else's firewood? What
about dragging your dissolution into small
claims Court Room Three, the incessant
February rain, the five minutes it took
to say *yes*, I am who I say I am; *yes*,
I married him; *yes*, I left. *Yes. Yes. No.*
What about all that, outside, afterwards,
soaked to the irreconcilable skin?

Conclusion

Picture this: A woman comes into my office
and sits in the orange plastic chair I've put there
for students. She's holding an essay, her first,
and she's "having some problems," she says.

I notice her lined pages tremble a little,
and her blue nail polish is chipped,
her fingers look raw. I look down
at my own hands, stained red
from canning beets, and I wonder
how I'll ever get them clean.
"I can't seem to finish," she says,
"I have no conclusion."

Picture this her essay says. *He didn't want
another man to have me. So he carved
his initials into my thigh. The scars never fade.*
It is precisely the picturing of this that is
the problem. I can't imagine
what it took to hold her down.

Mary, I want to say, two weeks before
she'll drop my class. *I'm having a hard time
picturing this.* But then I do. One person's will
against another: pinned wrists, a deliberate
cleaving. It is unbearably hot
in my pathetic office with stupid, orange chairs.

"How should I write a conclusion?" She asks again.

The conclusion? I picture myself, now, in class
the chalk dust settling on dark desktops.
Mary, I'm sorry I said the world could be made
neat in five paragraphs—beginning, middle and end.
That the simple placement of a comma
makes everything clear.

Today I picture this:
Mary's downtown, the roar
of Greyhounds surround her,
dust kicks up, catches the edge of her dress,
her shoulder droops from the weight of her bags,
sunlight on her bleached hair a halo.

Woman Outside The Golden Nugget

*"And stay out of the fucking room. I had money for the
bus, but you couldn't keep your hands off it . . ."*

Watch her make her way
through rows of slots their silver
slits ringing, whirring cherries,
bars, sevens. Each lobby's a maze of women
serving drinks: cheerleaders
at The Vegas Club, golden
goddesses at Caesar's.
Excalibur's Gueneviere balances
greyhounds, vodka tonics, J.D. neat.
Pass by the fake-fur camel's hump,
the humping thump of music, ring-ring,
hit me! hit me! Gold chains drip
over bobbing silicone sheathed
in leopard skin, spandex.
Roll on down green hallways,
like dice at craps—hard eight,
seven-eleven, line up your bets
with the other bridal parties.
Under stained glass of Canterbury,
give her the ring-ring. I do. I do.
I do. Buy her another round,
sweetie. Blow on the dice. Blow
on. Soon enough you'll roll

away from each other, honey.
Then you'll remember Vegas:
shows of lights, neon nights,
carnival feathers, iridescent
plastic jewels. Look, there
she is on hidden camera—your
bride. Now wait your turn.
Just one after
another. Just one more
for the road. Just one.
All right then, lean on in here,
she'll wait. Gimme some
luck. I'm running out
of here. I'm crack-cracking
the sidewalk near the faux falls
of the Oasis, the ships docked
at Treasure Island. Keep your hands
off me, hear? That's my treasure. Mine.

After His Affair

Her damp throat curved
soft before cool
belief. Bruised rib
tucked inside her
blouse, a sharp pain
blended with April air.

Wavering words
snapped red vowels
she bit like twists
of licorice.
Tell me, she said.
His eye upon the curve

of throat, he shifts
as he sits. Down
below river water,
rocks, mud
trippingly lift
twigs, bits of words and bone.

Sylvia Tries To Answer

No, I don't speak to the dead. I let them take
my tongue. I knew my hands would make their own
language. Besides, we have nothing to say
to each other in the haunting hereafter. Here,
words are dust motes barely perceptible.
The long thesaurus days, lists of synonyms, wasted.

Somehow I thought they would recognize the shape
of my emptiness and begin filling me. Then,
with their long fingers tracing my skin,
they might lace up what threatened to fly away.
Go to the page like a lover, but accept the world
of your body is elsewhere.

My mind was a damp series of rooms
I wandered in, dark, and no, I'm sorry,
I didn't think of them, their soft skin
and miniature hearts. I must have known
the fat gold watch of their lives
would continue without me.

What I wanted to say was despair wound
its way around me like morning glory,
its trumpeted blossoms stark and beautiful,

relentless tangling until my braceleted
arms no longer rose from my sides to wrap
around my babies or him. After a time,
there was simply no where to reach.

Writing wasn't enough. Nor loving either.

The Death of Them

She remembered fresh cut flowers
every week. Hand-tied bunches of purple irises,
white carnations or pink striped lilies
in a vase at the table's center. Whole handfuls
of yellow mums like suns framed by lacy ferns.
Once or twice, bouquets to work—
daisies with blue statice and a small card.

Then more flowers: wreaths and ornate
arrangements, cellophane-wrapped fuchsia
and baby's breath, birds of paradise, garish gladiolas—
rooms of flowers like funeral parlors. And the doorbell's ringing,
the deliveries, the constant maintenance—clipping the ends,
plucking the dead ones, the wilted brown
in varying stages of decay. She moved from room
to room, refilling the vases and jars with fresh water,
gathering up the mottled bunches, crushing
their wilted heads in a roar of disposal, breathing deeply
the death of them, the brackish, cloudy water's smell.

Flowers of consolation—a prize for waiting.
As she paced the beige carpet
to see his headlights cross the grass past midnight,
she noted yellow slits of luminescent irises
shivering under lamplight.

Falling

I
Long after you're gone
I listen for the evening
of your breath: the push and pull
of simple elements, the exchange
of murmur and hum. You think
a head injury makes you
twitch and jerk into sleep.
I think you are unwilling
to leave the world of plant and dig
to plunge fitfully to the place where
you cannot wish away
a father's death, a son's sadness,
weeks on the psych ward bed
curled behind the dark coma
of medication. *It's okay*, I whisper
to your convulsive limbs, your clenching jaw.
I hold you hard, as if to hold you together
as you fall away from me,
grinding your teeth against
whether or not you will wake.

II
After it was over,
I knew I was lucky.
I couldn't explain on the phone
thousands of miles from you,

in the space that lagged between
our words flung out across the Atlantic,
to the northern-most tip of Ireland
I'd crossed into Ulster to see.
I knew I shouldn't take my life
so lightly, stepping out to the unfamiliar
ledge, though I reached carefully
with my toes, testing the stones;
it wasn't enough. I knew
what was happening.
Suspended by time,
I recognized gravity,
knowing I couldn't stop it,
knowing I should want to.
After the tingling in my limbs,
I reached back to feel blood,
the rocks above the Irish Sea
beneath me. Right there,
I righted myself, knew that I hadn't
any more time than anyone else,
nor anything more to do.

Flight

Yesterday, as the sun set—
taut hot rays straight
in my eyes through the clouds
over the Safeway parking lot,
I carried three bags of groceries:
oranges and strawberries for breakfast,
avocados (three for a dollar), white corn
tortillas, cat food. I was smiling
because tulips were on sale—
$1.99 a bunch, and here they are
now on the table beside me, orange
waxy ruffles mixed with daffodils
about to burst. It didn't seem unusual,
any May first, when a warm loneliness
I thought was the sun, left my skin
flushed and tingling as I put the bags
in the passenger seat, the car into reverse,
and drove west.

It would've taken a mere slip of my foot
off the break as I neared the stop
at High Drive. Not even thirty seconds,
one for each year of my life, to press the gas,
push through the guardrail and with wings
finally feathered and wild, fly out
over the canyon. In flight long enough
to rise with the far canyon wall,

reach to the light, then turn and float
down. With the grace of hollow
bones, what would I be
thinking, staring past the sun?

Who am I kidding? I wouldn't think
of anything. I'd simply be happy for $1.99 tulips,
or any ordinary loneliness I could carry.

Notes

"Back To The Muse"— "I've been to four years of college, and. . ." is from Pam Houston's "Selway" in *Cowboys Are My Weakness.*

"What Children Hear" is after Jonathan Kozol's *Amazing Grace.*

"Just Before the Father Left" is for Missy.

"Becoming Santa" is for my father, Jim.

"Daytime Shatters Loose" is for my mother, Virginia.

"What We Do" is for Karen.

"From the Waitress Journals"—Wow! For Gail, Shannon, Shay, Karen, Shelley, Sofie, Stephanie, Jeanette, Ida, Lauren, Martha, Lynell, Pam, Candy, Rhonda, and the whole damn lot of you real and honorary waitresses.

Carolyn Forché's quote is from "The Visitor" in *The Country Between Us.*

"Loaded" is for Adam.